when you die you will not be scared to die

LINDSAY TUNKL

PARALLAX
PRESS

BERKELEY, CALIFORNIA

Parallax Press
P.O. Box 7355
Berkeley, California 94707
parallax.org

Parallax Press is the publishing division
of Plum Village Community of Engaged Buddhism, Inc.

Printed in Canada

Cover and text design by Jess Morphew
Author Photo © Kirsten Lara Getchell

Library of Congress Cataloging-in-Publication Data is available

ISBN: 978-1-941529-98-0

1 2 3 4 5 / 22 21 20 19 18

In endless loving memory of Vanessa Libertad Garcia
who taught me so much about being alive and fearless.

Contents

"To be mortal is the most basic human experience, and yet man has never been able to accept it, grasp it, and behave accordingly. Man doesn't know how to be mortal. And when he dies, he doesn't even know how to be dead."

MILAN KUNDERA,
Immortality

Meditations

PART ONE

I

When you die you will be free of fear.

When you die you will never have to wear clothes again.

When you die you will sleep forever.

When you die you will forget all about your fat.

When you die you will no longer feel guilty.

When you die you will forget that you got hurt.

When you die you will stop wondering if it was all worth it.

When you die you will be enough.

When you die you will stop thinking that you make bad art.

When you die you will let go of shame.

When you die you will forget to remember.

When you die you will not be scared to die.

2

When you die you won't judge yourself.

When you die you won't have to be alone.

When you die you won't worry about eating organic.

When you die you won't have to pick sides.

When you die you won't regret anything.

When you die you won't miss your ex.

When you die you won't need to work.

When you die you won't worry about the future.

When you die you won't remember pain.

When you die you won't need your mom.

When you die you won't forget anything important.

When you die you won't know you're dead.

3

When you die you will know everything you need to know.

When you die you will find peace.

When you die you will stop feeling bad about watching TV.

When you die you will be one with the Earth.

When you die you will stop fearing the apocalypse.

When you die you will finally know the ending.

When you die you will know that tomorrow doesn't matter.

When you die you will be free of anxiety.

When you die you will feel everything.

When you die you will be safe.

When you die you will be free of daddy issues.

When you die you will be present.

When you die you will not be scared to die.

4

When you die you won't be alone.

When you die you won't be preoccupied.

When you die you won't have to think about what to wear.

When you die you won't need for anything.

When you die you won't be concerned about tomorrow.

When you die you won't suffer any longer.

When you die you won't blame yourself.

When you die you won't try to understand why.

When you die you won't care about time.

When you die you won't obsess about black holes.

When you die you won't care about romance.

When you die you won't know you're dead.

5

When you die you will know what love feels like.

When you die you will be whole.

When you die you will not care about getting likes.

When you die you will stop fearing the unknown.

When you die you will have everything you need.

When you die you will have enough money.

When you die you will know everything you need to know.

When you die you will never have to pee again.

When you die you will reach the event horizon.

When you die you will just be.

When you die you will not worry about getting cancer.

When you die you will not be scared to die.

6

When you die you won't need to question anything.

When you die you won't feel envy.

When you die you won't want to stalk anyone on Facebook.

When you die you won't try to be anything you're not.

When you die you won't waste any time.

When you die you won't take anything for granted.

When you die you won't believe in aliens.

When you die you won't let anyone down.

When you die you won't miss a thing.

When you die you won't need to meditate.

When you die you won't have to buy tampons.

When you die you won't know you're dead.

7

When you die you will be honest.

When you die you will never be hungry.

When you die you will be free.

When you die you will have done the best you could.

When you die you will stop complicating things.

When you die you will rest.

When you die you will never binge-watch anything again.

When you die you will stop avoiding love.

When you die you will have a hard body.

When you die you will have all the time you need.

When you die you will be one with the ocean.

When you die you will not be scared to die.

8

When you die you won't overthink things.

When you die you won't break any promises.

When you die you won't contribute to climate change.

When you die you won't be alone.

When you die you won't care about your cracked cuticles.

When you die you won't feel bad about eating pizza.

When you die you won't be addicted to anything.

When you die you won't ever fail.

When you die you won't hurt anyone's feelings.

When you die you won't be held accountable.

When you die you won't second-guess yourself.

When you die you won't know you're dead.

9

When you die you will be free of capitalist desires.

When you die you will let go of expectations.

When you die you will forgive.

When you die you will understand "forever."

When you die you will let go of your insecurities.

When you die you will stop rushing.

When you die you will never have to wear pantyhose.

When you die you will stop judging people.

When you die you will be still.

When you die you will be fearless.

When you die you will be held by the earth.

When you die you will not be scared to die.

10

When you die you won't be resentful.

When you die you won't feel scared of doors left ajar.

When you die you won't look for the flaws.

When you die you won't be impatient.

When you die you won't lie to yourself.

When you die you won't cling to realism.

When you die you won't need to learn how to love.

When you die you won't feel guilty about smoking.

When you die you won't obsessively make lists.

When you die you won't think about your bad tattoos.

When you die you won't go to empty wells for water.

When you die you won't know you're dead.

II

When you die you will let down your shields.

When you die you will stop measuring distance.

When you die you will be eulogized.

When you die you will put down your phone.

When you die you will stop looking for lost items.

When you die you will not be pretending.

When you die you will understand death.

When you die you will proceed.

When you die you will confront death.

When you die you will forget about living.

When you die you will not mumble.

When you die you will not be scared to die.

12

When you die you won't wait.

When you die you won't get lost.

When you die you won't need hope.

When you die you won't be pressured to hike.

When you die you won't have unreasonable expectations.

When you die you won't spend time critiquing.

When you die you won't disappoint anyone.

When you die you won't be late.

When you die you won't procrastinate.

When you die you won't worry about your looks.

When you die you won't get embarrassed.

When you die you won't know you're dead.

"Why didn't I learn to treat everything like it was the last time? My greatest regret was how much I believed in the future."

JONATHAN SAFRAN FOER,
Extremely Loud and Incredibly Close

Meditations

PART TWO

13

When you die you won't be scared of heights.

When you die you won't search for a better comeback.

When you die you won't have trust issues.

When you die you won't be angry.

When you die you won't bring your baggage with you.

When you die you won't mind waiting.

When you die you won't feel powerless.

When you die you won't need anymore.

When you die you won't wonder if you're crazy.

When you die you won't have to check your email.

When you die you won't be haunted.

When you die you won't know you're dead.

14

When you die you will have slept more than enough hours.

When you die you will forget all the times you felt humiliated.

When you die you will stop wondering about reincarnation.

When you die you will act your age.

When you die you will never screen calls.

When you die you will be free of debt.

When you die you will know the truth about ghosts.

When you die you will begin something else.

When you die you will be a heartbreaker.

When you die you will ignore nothing.

When you die you will disregard everything.

When you die you will not be scared to die.

15

When you die you won't care about being right.

When you die you won't have trouble sleeping.

When you die you won't need a massage.

When you die you won't check your bank balance.

When you die you won't forget your best friend's birthday.

When you die you won't care who sees you naked.

When you die you won't have to go to weddings.

When you die you won't wear sunscreen.

When you die you won't pay taxes.

When you die you won't be confused by the electoral college.

When you die you won't cry when you watch the news.

When you die you won't know you're dead.

16

When you die you will know control is an illusion.
When you die you will see that death is exaggerated.
When you die you will let go of urgency.
When you die you will feel limitless.
When you die you will stop comparing.
When you die you will lose all your credit cards.
When you die you will make peace with discomfort.
When you die you will stop wondering about chances you
didn't take.
When you die you will be cold blooded.
When you die you will feel what it feels like to feel nothing.
When you die you will be someone's first experience of death.
When you die you will not be scared to die.

17

When you die you won't have road rage.

When you die you won't be confused about wanting kids.

When you die you won't miss people you can't find.

When you die you won't feel ashamed of your kinks.

When you die you won't be too emotional.

When you die you won't need glasses.

When you die you won't be a hypochondriac.

When you die you won't have headaches.

When you die you won't visit gravestones.

When you die you won't need an emergency kit.

When you die you won't need comforting.

When you die you won't know you're dead.

18

When you die you will forget your own birthday.

When you die you will stop watching the clock.

When you die you will reach the peak of self-improvement.

When you die you will find a permanent solution.

When you die you will be free of all curses.

When you die you will never feel the pain of unrequited love.

When you die you will have plenty of alone time.

When you die you will lose all your wrinkles.

When you die you will stop searching.

When you die you will break down.

When you die you will always be there.

When you die you will not be scared to die.

19

When you die you won't need a haircut.

When you die you won't feel ashamed of watching porn.

When you die you won't need antidepressants.

When you die you won't awkwardly hug people you don't
want to hug.

When you die you won't sit by the phone waiting for her call.

When you die you won't fail at love.

When you die you won't question the accuracy of memory.

When you die you won't waste time.

When you die you won't watch what you eat.

When you die you won't have to reckon with the opinions
of others.

When you die you won't need a meaningful philosophy of life.

When you die you won't know you're dead.

20

When you die you will stop clearing the wreckage.

When you die you will know how it all ends.

When you die you will let it go.

When you die you will stop waiting for something better.

When you die you will take your final breath.

When you die you will follow in your father's footsteps.

When you die you will turn to dust.

When you die you will have done it all.

When you die you will stop fighting.

When you die you will forget about time.

When you die you will be well on your way.

When you die you will not be scared to die.

21

When you die you won't be confused about day-to-day reality.
When you die you won't sit through superficial conversations.
When you die you won't get any older.
When you die you won't get chub rub.
When you die you won't have deadlines.
When you die you won't need a therapist, a dentist,
  or a lawyer.
When you die you won't be a flake.
When you die you won't care about your failings.
When you die you won't feel trapped.
When you die you won't think that life is all about you.
When you die you won't care what happens next.
When you die you won't know you're dead.

22

When you die you will know infinity.

When you die you will breathe a little lighter.

When you die you will stop loving people who aren't
good for you.

When you die you will stop being a cynic.

When you die you will receive kindness from others.

When you die you will stop thinking about the end.

When you die you will turn blue.

When you die you will never be ghosted.

When you die you will never need coffee.

When you die you will never lose your keys.

When you die you will cross over.

When you die you will not be scared to die.

23

When you die you won't be scared to dance alone.

When you die you won't resist fate.

When you die you won't care about being normal.

When you die you won't take any of it with you.

When you die you won't know the difference.

When you die you won't have to use condoms.

When you die you won't wonder if love is forever.

When you die you won't take out the trash.

When you die you won't have to split the check.

When you die you won't have to shit in public.

When you die you won't long for better days.

When you die you won't know you're dead.

24

When you die you will stop being afraid.

When you die you will finally commit.

When you die you will never have to apologize.

When you die you will have accomplished all that you could.

When you die you will stop overanalyzing.

When you die you will not be embarrassed by your body.

When you die you will know finality.

When you die you will grasp that time is relative.

When you die you will know that nothing lives forever.

When you die you will see that failure is fine.

When you die you will be right on time.

When you die you will not be scared to die.

"As loss reinvents itself so does love.
There is no freeing ourselves from either.
The creativity of love needs the pain of loss.
With nothing to risk, love can't exist."

DARIO ROBLETO,

Lunge for Love as If It Were Air

Afterword

I wrestle with a profound fear of death. My fear is not unique by any means, but it is my own. I am terrified of losing the people I love and dying before I have lived a "full" life. At times, my fear of dying has resembled the pain I feel when I look at my lover, a perfectly imperfect being I'd never want to live without. I already anticipate the ending of such a great love. I am already mourning, drowning with grief, at the thought of parting ways with this person. In those moments, overcome with a loss that has yet to occur, I am inconsolable. I am inconsolable in the same way when I think about dying. I am already mourning my own passing, missing out on living, yearning for the people I love.

Yet death is not like that. Most likely, death is like nothing. It feels like nothing. It requires nothing. I will not even know I am dead. Then why am I so scared to die? For me this is a question I do not expect to answer, but it has driven years of research and creative exploration. The burden of our uncertain existence is an opportunity to examine the simultaneous simplicity and complexity of our humanness.

Humans have the ability to feel complex physical sensations and emotions and then process them cognitively. Because of this, we aren't solely motivated by instinct or the need to survive. We can make choices that can hinder or support our survival. Our ability to feel and process our feelings affects our relationship to death. In his book *Psychology of Death*, Robert Kaustenbaum points out that because we cannot possibly know what it feels like not to feel (for not feeling anything would mean death), our relationship to death and the dead is immediately placed in opposition to life and the living. This opposition can be terrifying.

* * *

As an artist, a would-be philosopher, a seeker, and a rabbit hole chaser, I have made it my life's work to move toward the things that scare me the most. In a move toward the chasm that sits between me as a living person and me as a dead person, I asked myself to consider if there was a way to reframe death as something to look forward to. I began thinking of the benefits that might come along with death, and the first list emerged:

When you die you will be free of fear.
When you die you will never have to shop at the Gap again.
When you die you will sleep forever.
When you die you will forget all about your fat.
When you die you will no longer feel guilty.
When you die you will forget that you got hurt.
When you die you will stop wondering if it was all worth it.

When you die you will be enough.
When you die you will stop thinking that you make bad art.
When you die you will let go of shame.
When you die you will forget to remember.
When you die you will not be scared to die.

* * *

What landed on the page was a list of fears and difficulties I was dealing with in that moment, and the promise that I would be free of those things were I to die. Some were cliché, some were embarrassing, and some were miniscule in the scheme of things. But each one felt meaningful somehow. When I die I won't have fear, or guilt, or shame because I will no longer have access to my dynamic humanness. I also won't think about my fat or shop at the Gap, where the clothes don't fit me well, or question my value because of my body or what goes on or in it.

These simple truths felt like a huge relief, and as I continued writing my perception of death started to change. At the same time, I began to come to terms with the triviality of those things that haunt me and make me less present for living.

The first twelve poems were written one poem a day with little to no editing and the parameter that they had to be "objectively" true. There is no guarantee of objectivity when it comes to death, which is one of the reasons it scares me so much, but I worked with that ambition in mind. As I wrote, I began to feel relief. Total strangers and my closest confidants who read the meditations told me that they also began to feel relief. We laughed about death, cried about death, and most importantly, we played within the nuances of dying.

I went back and forth for a couple of years about whether to write more meditations. I didn't want them to become redundant or lose their meaning. I didn't want to mess up a good thing. But I believed that there was more to explore about death and its gifts. I wrote the twelve poems in the second part with a very different process. I let myself edit, and I bent the rule of objective truth when it felt important. Some resonate on the same level as the first twelve, and some are more philosophical and up for debate. My hope is that these poems allow even more space for thought and intimate connection around death and our fear of it. I hope that those who have never looked at death directly will take a glance. I hope that those who are soon facing death feel comfort. I hope that those who are feeling the loss of another can feel it with open arms, reminded that the weight of their despair is directly proportional to the weight of their love.

Is it possible to be truly fearless in the face of ultimate uncertainty? I don't know. As a living person, do I still miss those that I love who have left this plane? Absolutely. The frustrations, annoyances, pains, and tragedies of the day-to-day continue to pull me in and out of focus with what really matters. I still have a lot to learn and, hopefully, possibly, a long way to go, but I rest a little easier when I remember that when I die I will not be scared to die.

Lindsay Tunkl
Oakland, California, Fall 2017

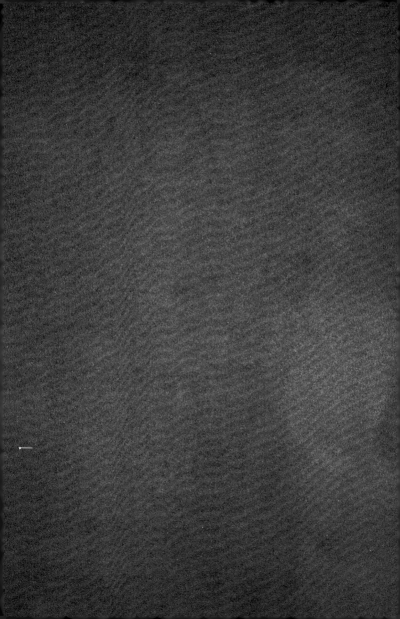

Recommended Reading

Barthes, Roland. *Camera Lucida*. Translated by Richard Howard. New York: Hill and Wang, 1980.

Camera Lucida is a moving and emotional exploration of how photography relates to many facets of the human condition, including death. In particular, Barthes examines his relationship to his deceased mother through the photographs that remain.

Butler, Judith. *Precarious Life: The Powers of Mourning and Violence*. New York: Verso, 2004.

Precarious Life is one of the most important books I've read. It examines death, mourning and violence in relation to the world at large and the political climate. In a testament to the merger of the political and the personal, Butler explores how loss is transformative if we let it be.

Critchley, Simon. *Notes on Suicide*. London: Fitzcarraldo Editions, 2015.

Critchley challenges many conventional ideas about suicide while abandoning moral judgement and examining suicide with intriguing and thoughtful consideration.

Didion, Joan. *The Year of Magical Thinking*. New York: Knopf, 2005.

This acclaimed book is an invitation to enter Didion's mind after the loss of a great love in the midst of tremendous grief. I strive towards the North Star of Didion's bravery and radical honesty.

Freud, Sigmund. *Mourning and Melancholia: 1917*. Rahway: Merck, Sharp & Dohme, 1972.

While Freud's methods and theories are questionable, his works created a foundation for a vast amount of contemporary psychological exploration. This particular piece is a beautiful and devastating examination of those who survive loss.

Garcia, Vanessa Libertad. *The Voting Booth after Dark: Despicable, Embarrassing, Repulsive.* Los Angeles: Fiat Libertad, 2009.

Vanessa Libertad Garcia was one of the brightest humans I have ever met. She was a queer Latina writer and filmmaker whose bravery and gumption inspired many. She committed suicide in 2014 and left a big hole in the hearts of many. Her book of poetry and essays about a troubled group of young club kids in Los Angeles in the time proceeding and around the 2008 United States elections is dark, moving, and more relevant now than ever before.

Ishiguro, Kazuo. *Never Let Me Go*. New York: Vintage, 2006.

Kazuo's book is a sci-fi portrait of a future in which humanity has made surviving natural death their main priority. While following a few people as they live their lives in this society, Ishiguro paints a beautiful and disturbing portrait of what might happen when the value of human life and death shifts beyond what we know it now to be.

Kastenbaum, Robert. *The Psychology of Death.* New York: Springer, 2006.

The Psychology of Death is an academic text, but is written beautifully and has informed the way I think about death.

Kundera, Milan. *The Unbearable Lightness of Being*. New York: Harper and Row, 1984.

Kundera uses fascinating characters to ask a myriad of existential questions regarding the meaning of life. Set in Prague in 1968, the book examines how these characters live their lives in the event and shadow of the Prague Spring.

Levine, Stephen. *A Year to Live: How to Live This Year as If It Were Your Last*. New York: Bell Tower, 1998.

This book is both a philosophical exploration of our fear of death and an instruction manual for a meditation practice. The year-long meditation practice leads participants through living a year of your life as if it were your last. Even if you don't follow the meditation program, it's a powerful book.

McCarthy, Tom, Simon Critchley, and Leah Whitman-Salkin. *The Mattering of Matter: Documents from the Archive of the International Necronautical Society*. Berlin: Sternberg, 2012.

The International Necronautical Society is a group of writers and philosophers who examine death as a "space" that can be mapped, navigated, and examined. Through the investigation of art, literature, surfing, and many other practices, this book digs deep into death and its possibilities.

Nietzsche, Friedrich. *The Gay Science: With a Prelude in German Rhymes and an Appendix of Songs*. Translated by Walter Kaufmann. New York: Vintage, 1974. Originally published in 1882.

Nietzsche, often hailed as a nihilist and a pessimist, may have been those things at some moments in his life, but he was also an optimist who had many brilliant ideas of how to live life with presence, acceptance, and bounty.

About the Author

What does it mean to be human in the contemporary moment, when everything is seemingly tragic and absurd at the same time? It is Lindsay Tunkl's aim to create spaces for this question to be answered, for the individual and for the human species. By researching and exploring subjects such as Affect, Death, the Apocalypse, Encounter, Solitude, Space, and Time, Tunkl's tender and humorous work invites the viewer into reflective experiences with their emotions, their perspectives, and their place within a world that is often heartbreaking.

Tunkl graduated from California College of the Arts in San Francisco with an MFA in Interdisciplinary Studio Practice and an MA in Visual + Critical Studies in 2017, and received a BFA from CalArts in Los Angeles in 2010.

Her work has been shown in the United States and internationally, most notably at: the Hammer Museum, Los Angeles; Southern Exposure, San Francisco; the Center for Contemporary Arts, Santa Fe; and Performance Space, London.

Also by Lindsay Tunkl

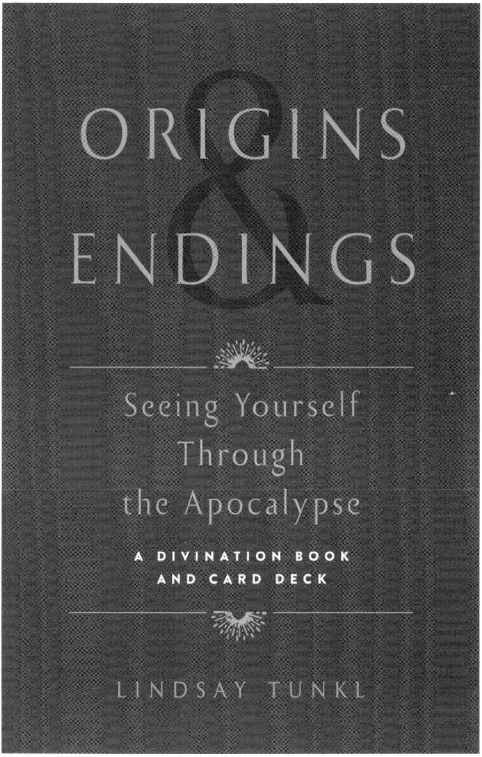
ORIGINS
&
ENDINGS
Seeing Yourself
Through
the Apocalypse
A DIVINATION BOOK
AND CARD DECK
LINDSAY TUNKL

PARALLAX
PRESS

Parallax Press is a nonprofit publisher, founded and inspired by Zen Master Thich Nhat Hanh. We publish books on mindfulness in daily life and are committed to making these teachings accessible to everyone and preserving them for future generations. We do this work to alleviate suffering and contribute to a more just and joyful world.

For a copy of the catalog, please contact:

Parallax Press
P.O. Box 7355
Berkeley, CA 94707
parallax.org